SHOPPING THEN AND NOW

Joy Brewster

Contents

Getting the Goods

Where does your family go to buy milk or bread? Where do you go to buy a new pair of shoes? Today, there are **supermarkets, malls,** and many other places where we can get the **goods** we need.

That wasn't always so easy. The Pilgrims came to America from England almost 400 years ago. They had to grow most of their food and make their own clothes. Ships brought shoes, metal tools, and other things they needed all the way across the Atlantic Ocean.

Trading for furs

The Pilgrims also got some goods from Native Americans. The Pilgrims took knives, beads, and other trinkets to meeting places called **trading posts.** They traded the knives and trinkets for warm furs from animals that Native Americans hunted.

You could call those early trading posts the first American stores. You are about to find out how we got from those first stores to the malls and supermarkets where we shop today!

Early American Shops

More and more settlers came to America. They built towns, and started to make things that they needed right in the towns. Blacksmiths made iron tools, nails, and cooking pots. Carpenters built furniture. Cobblers made shoes. Some of these **craftspeople** set up shops to sell the things they made.

Blacksmith

By the 1700s, most towns had different shops or places to get goods. You might buy a hat from the hatmaker, or sugar from the grocer.

If you needed fruit or eggs, you could stop by the market on the town square and buy some from a farmer. The market was a busy place where farmers sold their goods. It was also a popular place to gather. You might see a puppet show, a footrace, dancing—even a pig-chasing contest!

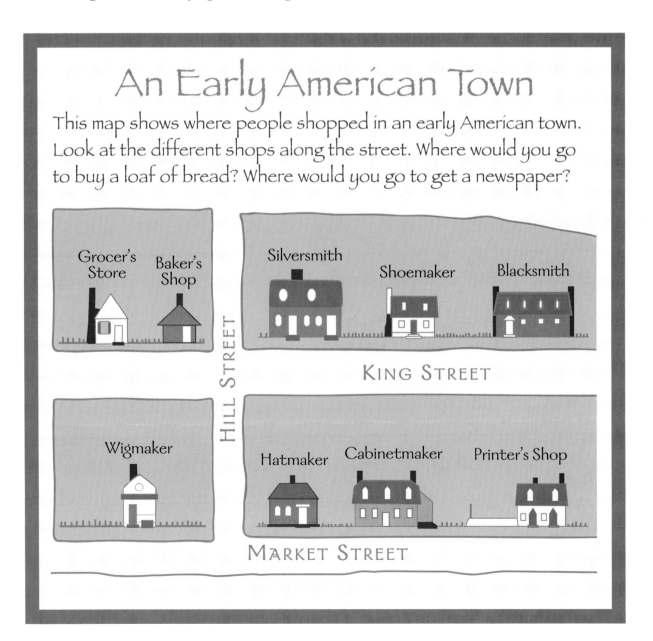

An Early American Town

This map shows where people shopped in an early American town. Look at the different shops along the street. Where would you go to buy a loaf of bread? Where would you go to get a newspaper?

Grocer's Store　Baker's Shop

Silversmith　Shoemaker　Blacksmith

HILL STREET

KING STREET

Wigmaker

Hatmaker　Cabinetmaker　Printer's Shop

MARKET STREET

Workers like this man once used wood to make wheels for horse-drawn carriages.

Most of the time people paid for goods by trading things they grew or made themselves. A farmer could trade corn or apples for other things at the market. Some people traded their **services.** That means they did something for someone else in exchange for what they wanted. A shoemaker might fix a blacksmith's boots in exchange for some nails the blacksmith made. But sometimes people used money instead of trading.

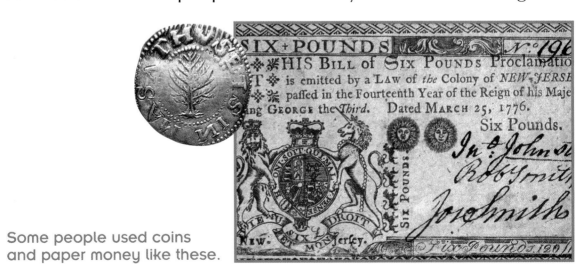

Some people used coins and paper money like these.

People who lived out in the country had a harder time getting things they needed. Many people had to wait for **peddlers** to come to their homes. These salesmen walked or rode from door to door. They sold things they carried on their backs or in wagons. They sold household goods such as pots, buttons, combs, and tools.

Peddler

People paid the peddler by trading things such as furs, soap, and food. Sometimes the peddler's load was even heavier on his way back home!

Shopping Today

Small Shops

Today, some places have small shops like the ones in early American towns. And like the early stores, these shops sell things that are made by hand.

General Stores

Two hundred years after the Pilgrims first came to America, many people still grew a lot of their own food. But they needed to buy things such as spices and coffee. In small towns and in **rural** areas far from cities, the general store was the only place to shop.

People could get just about anything they needed at a general store. Shelves were packed with everything from soap to schoolbooks. Countertops held jars of penny candy. Barrels of flour and coffee stood on the floor. Pots hung from the ceiling.

General store

General stores sold things like pots and pans.

Owners of general stores ordered some of their goods from far away. But many things came from farmers and people who lived nearby. For example, a craftsperson in town might make the soap that was sold at the general store.

A few people paid for goods with money, but most traded. A farm family might trade butter and eggs for things they couldn't make at home. Then the general store would sell the butter and eggs to people who lived in town.

This girl is bringing eggs from her family's farm to trade for things she needs.

In rural areas, people lived far apart. Many people had to walk or drive a horse and wagon a long way to the general store. Often people made the trip only once or twice a month. For them, a trip to the general store was a big event. Sometimes it was their only chance to see neighbors.

The general store was more than a place to buy things. People met there to talk, hear news, play games, and chat about the season's crops. Sometimes, the general store was also the bank and the post office.

For most of the 1800s, many Americans got everything they needed from the local general store. But the way people shopped was about to change.

Shopping Today

General Stores

Some towns in rural areas still have general stores, like this one in Vermont. Today, most people drive cars to the general store.

Mail-Order Catalogs

At the end of the 1800s, parts of the United States were getting crowded. Some people went to start farms in places where no one else lived yet. These farmers were far away from the closest general store. It was hard for them to get the things they needed.

Mail-Order Catalogs

Sometimes salesmen traveled to farms to sell goods to farmers. One salesman was a young man named Aaron Montgomery Ward. Farmers told him that they wanted more things to buy and cheaper prices. Ward came up with the idea of **mail-order catalogs.** The catalogs offered people things at very low prices. Soon, other people copied Ward's idea.

Rural families called catalogs "wish books."

The catalogs showed hundreds of pictures of farming supplies and household goods. A farmer could order a plow, a hammer, or a wagon. His wife could order a sewing machine, a rolling pin, or a pretty hat. People didn't have to travel anywhere to get what they needed. They just had to put their orders in the mail. When the goods came, people picked them up at the closest railroad station to their home.

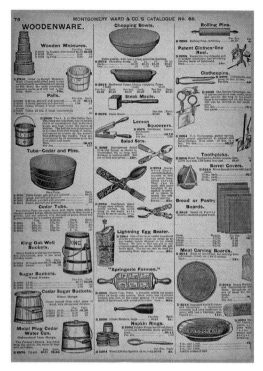

Shopping Today

Catalogs

Today, lots of people still shop with catalogs. And today, shopping with a catalog is much easier. It's much faster, too. Can you guess why?

New Stores for Cities

Shopping in cities was easier than shopping in rural areas. People in cities lived near different kinds of shops. But shopping in cities started to change, too.

Macy's **department store** takes up a whole block in New York City. This photo shows the store in the early 1900s.

Department Stores

A new kind of store opened in large cities like New York and Chicago. The new stores were big. They sold many different things. These stores were called department stores because they kept items in separate sections, or departments. There might be a department for girls' dresses, one for men's hats, and another one for pots and pans.

Shopping at a department store was a little like shopping in a general store, but department stores were much fancier. Shoppers were treated like special guests. There was entertainment, such as piano concerts. Many department stores also had restaurants right in the store. Department stores soon became popular places to meet friends and spend the day.

Five-and-Tens

The trouble with department stores was that their prices were high. Many people could not afford to shop in them. A new kind of store gave people another choice.

Can you imagine selling everything in a store for just five or ten cents? That's what F. W. Woolworth decided to do when he opened the first "five-and-ten" store.

The five-and-ten was very different from a department store. There was nothing fancy about it, and people who didn't want to spend a lot of money could shop there.

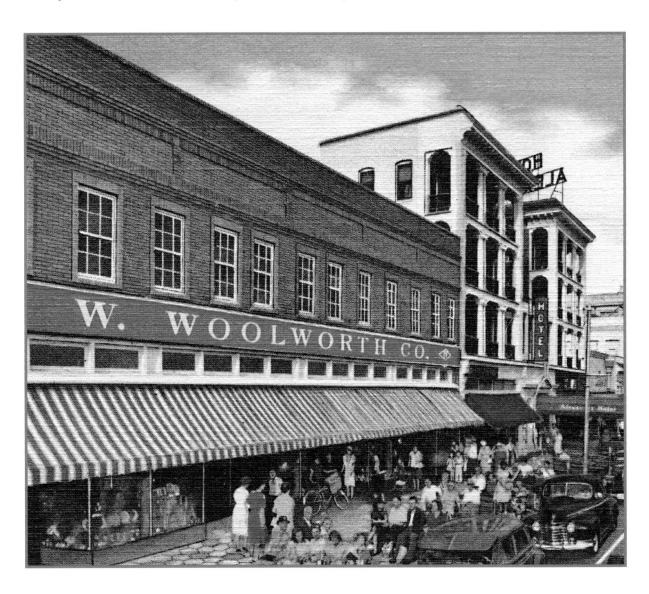

Almost everything in a five-and-ten cost either five or ten cents.

Five-and-tens sold all sorts of household goods like thread, paper, dishes, and kitchen tools. People liked the choice of goods and the low prices. Kids loved the candy and toys.

Shopping Today

Five-and-Tens

Five-and-ten stores are not around today. But there are still stores where you can buy everything for one low price.

Grocery Stores to Supermarkets

In the early 1900s, people in cities and big towns bought food at grocery stores. They weren't like grocery stores we have today. They didn't sell every kind of food. Shoppers had to get meat, bread, and vegetables from different small shops, such as butcher shops and bakeries. People also didn't do their own shopping. They gave lists of the things they wanted to **clerks** in the grocery stores. The clerks got the items from the shelves and wrapped them. Then other workers delivered the food to people's homes.

Then bigger grocery stores opened. They were called "self-service" stores. People could choose their own goods right from the shelf. Owners of self-service stores could sell things for lower prices because they didn't have to pay so many clerks.

By the 1950s, supermarkets were more like the ones we shop in today.

In the 1930s, the first supermarkets opened. The new stores were large, but they weren't fancy at all. Food was stacked on empty boxes instead of shelves. Shoppers didn't mind because the prices were low.

Shoppers also liked the new supermarkets because they sold meat, milk, bread, and fruit and vegetables. Now people could get all their food at one place.

Shopping Today

Supermarkets

Today, supermarkets are bigger than ever. Shoppers have even more choices. You might find six different kinds of apples, or 20 kinds of cereal.

Shopping Centers to Malls

In the 1940s and 1950s, people started moving out of towns and cities to the **suburbs.** A suburb is a community that is just outside a city. Soon, **shopping centers** opened in the suburbs. A shopping center usually had stores, a post office, a bank, and a parking lot. People walked outside to get from one place to another.

Then a new kind of shopping center called a mall became popular. Malls were located where there was plenty of land for big buildings and parking lots.

Most malls today have a department store and lots of other stores, too—all indoors under one roof. Shoppers can walk from store to store without stepping outside. The mall is the perfect place for one-stop shopping.

Malls are more than places to shop. Teenagers like to hang out there with friends. Families can go to a mall to have dinner and see a movie. Older people stroll along the walkways for exercise.

Busy Americans are still looking for new ways to save money and time. One new way to shop is the Internet. We can buy almost anything **on-line,** such as groceries, books, clothes, and music. We can "visit" a store without leaving home.

What will shopping be like in the future? You can be pretty sure that shoppers will keep looking for the best products, the lowest prices, and the easiest ways to shop.

How Shopping Has Changed

Kinds of Goods	Where People Shopped Long Ago	Where We Shop Today
Bread	Baker's shop	Baker's shop Grocery store Supermarket
Cooking pot	Blacksmith's shop Peddler General store Mail-order catalog Five-and-ten	Mail-order catalog Department store Mall Internet
Eggs	Market on town square General store Grocery store	Grocery store Supermarket
Shoes	Shoemaker's shop Mail-order catalog Department store	Mail-order catalog Department store Mall Internet
Soap	Peddler General store Five-and-ten	Grocery store Supermarket Mall

Glossary

clerk a person who helps customers in a store

craftsperson a person who makes things by hand

department store a large store that sells things in separate sections or departments

goods products that are sold

mail-order catalog a booklet of items that can be bought and delivered by mail

mall a large shopping area or building with many stores connected by walkways

on-line available on the Internet or World Wide Web

peddler a person who travels from place to place to sell things

rural having to do with the country

service work that helps other people

shopping center a group of stores and services with a parking lot

suburb a community located just outside a city

supermarket a large store that sells groceries and household items

trading post a place where people can trade local products for other goods